Using Ramps and Wedges

Wendy Sadler

www.raintreepublishers.co.uk
Visit our website to find out more information about **Raintree** books.

To order:
☎ Phone 44 (0) 1865 888112
📄 Send a fax to 44 (0) 1865 314091
💻 Visit the Raintree Bookshop at **www.raintreepublishers.co.uk** to browse our catalogue and order online.

First published in Great Britain by Raintree, Halley Court, Jordan Hill, Oxford, OX2 8EJ, part of Harcourt Education.
Raintree is a registered trademark of Harcourt Education Ltd.

Editorial: Melanie Copland and Kate Buckingham
Design: Michelle Lisseter, Victoria Bevan and Bridge Creative Services Ltd
Picture Research: Hannah Taylor
Production: Duncan Gilbert

Originated by Repro Multi Warna
Printed and bound in China by South China Printing Company

ISBN 1 844 43604 7
09 08 07 06 05
10 9 8 7 6 5 4 3 2 1

British Library Cataloguing in Publication Data
Sadler, Wendy
Using Ramps and Wedges. – (Machines Inside Machines)
621.9'92
A full catalogue record for this book is available from the British Library.

Acknowledgements
The publishers would like to thank the following for permission to reproduce photographs:
Alamy Images (Photofusion Picture Library) p. 10; Corbis pp. 17, 28; Corbis (Sygma/ Daemmrich Bob) p. 9; Corbis (Amos Nachoum) p. 26; Corbis (Bo Zaunders) p. 4; Corbis (Bruce Miller) p. 25; Corbis (David Aubrey) p. 20; Corbis (Gunter Marx) p. 24; Corbis (Lester Lefkowitz) p. 14; Corbis (NewSport) p. 5; Corbis (Raymond Gehman) p. 19; Getty Images (Imagebank) pp. 27, 29; Getty Images/Stone p. 11; Harcourt Education Ltd (Tudor Photography) pp. 6, 8, 12, 15, 16, 18, 21, 22; REX Features pp. 7, 13.

Cover photograph of zip reproduced with permission of Getty Images/ The Image Bank.

Every effort has been made to contact copyright holders of any material reproduced in this book. Any omissions will be rectified in subsequent printings if notice is given to the publishers.

The paper used to print this book comes from sustainable resources

Contents

Any words appearing in the text in bold,
like this, are explained in the glossary.

Machines with ramps and wedges

If you look around you every day you can see ramps and **wedges** in action. Cars are driven on to ferries using ramps. Aeroplanes are held in place at the airport using wedges behind the wheels. You use two wedges when you cut paper using scissors.

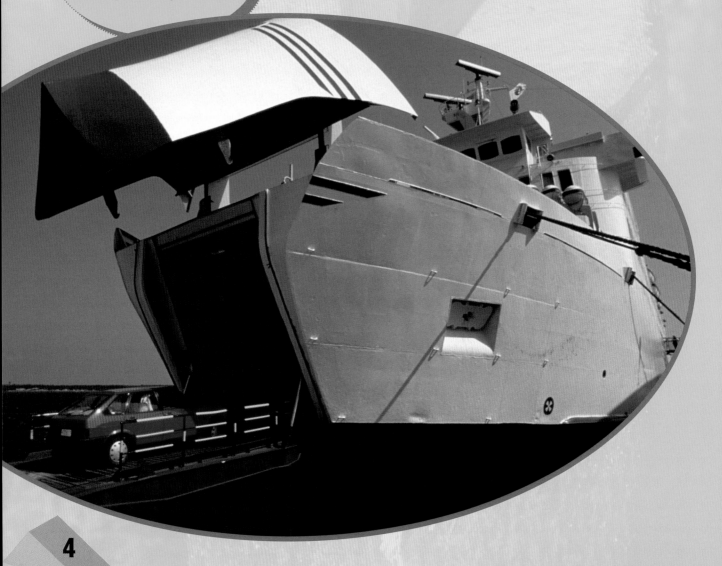

This car is being driven on to a ferry using a ramp.

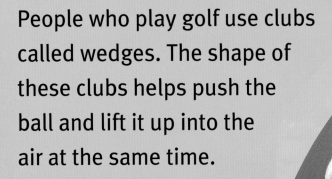

People who play golf use clubs called wedges. The shape of these clubs helps push the ball and lift it up into the air at the same time.

Ramps and wedges are both slopes that help us do things. They are very simple, but very important.

Wedges are used in golf to lift the ball up into the air.

What is a ramp?

A ramp is a **simple machine** that helps us to move things in a **vertical** direction (up or down). A ramp is a slope, which means a flat surface that has one end higher than the other.

A ramp makes an **angle** with the ground like the corner of a triangle. Ramps are also called **inclined planes**.

A skateboard rolls easily up and down a ramp.

Imagine trying to slide a heavy box up a ramp. It would be quite difficult because the box and the ramp would rub together. This rubbing is a **force** called **friction**. It makes it harder to push the box up the slope. If some wheels were added to the box there would be much less friction. This means it would be easier to move the box up the ramp.

These boxes have been put on a trolley. The trolley has wheels which make it easier to pull the boxes up the ramp.

Activity

Put the palms of your hands together and rub them forwards and backwards as fast as you can. There is friction between your hands. What does it feel like?

How do ramps help us?

When you need to move something from one place to another it takes work. The work you do is a mixture of the **effort force** you put in, and the distance you want the object to move.

Effort force is how much you have to push or pull. If you need to lift a heavy box straight up in the air you are moving a small distance but you need to use a lot of effort force.

Lifting a heavy box can be very hard to do and can be dangerous even for adults. You should never lift up heavy boxes.

When you use a ramp, you move the box a longer distance because the length of the slope is more than the height of the ramp. You have to push the box further, but the effort force you use is less. This makes the job a lot easier. A longer ramp will make the slope less steep, which makes the job even easier to do.

height of ramp

length of slope

The length of the slope is bigger than the height you need to lift the heavy object.

Ramps all around you

Some vehicles have ramps as well as steps up to the door. The ramp helps people using pushchairs and wheelchairs to get on to the vehicle.

The distance up a ramp is more than the distance up a set of steps, but because a ramp has a smooth slope, wheels can roll up it. A ramp cannot be too steep or it would be too hard to get up and too fast coming down.

It would be very hard work trying to get a wheelchair on to this bus without a ramp.

Ramps in hills

San Francisco in the USA has lots of steep hills. Some of the hills are too steep for cars to drive up and down. One street uses ramps in the road to help people climb the hill. Each bit of the road climbs a small amount of the hill at a time by zigzagging across it.

These ramps make the cars drive a longer distance, but make it easier and safer to drive down the hill.

Ramps in machines

Not all ramps help you climb hills. On a hot day they can also help you cool down. The blades on a fan are ramps. The ramps are joined on to a wheel and **axle** so that they can spin round. As they turn round the ramps push air forwards.

A fan is a **compound machine** because it uses at least two **simple machines** together.

If you look at a fan from the side you can see the slopes of the blades.

When you go on an escalator you are moving up or down a ramp. Stairs are a type of ramp as well, even though they do not a have a smooth slope. You travel a longer distance by going up stairs or an escalator, but you can climb very high. You could not climb this high in just one big step!

An escalator carries you up or down a ramp without you having to climb it yourself.

Ramps for fun

The ramps on a roller coaster carry you quickly up and down over very large distances. Sometimes you are pulled up the first slope by wheels, **pulleys,** and an **engine**. Then the **force** of **gravity** makes the roller coaster move downwards.

A roller coaster uses ramps, wheels, and pulleys to give you an exciting ride!

If the roller coaster fell straight down it would land with a very large bump. The ramps let the roller coaster move down more gently and safely.

14

Some unusual clocks use ramps to tell us the time. Metal balls roll down ramps inside the clock. Each ball takes a certain time to roll down the ramps. The number of balls at the bottom tells us how much time has gone by.

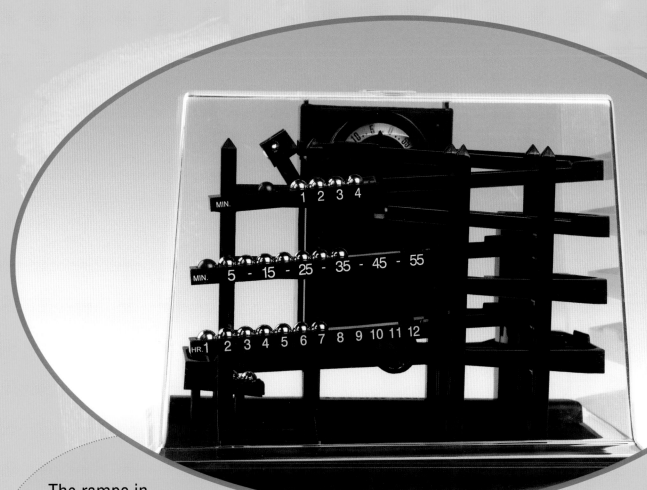

The ramps in this clock are important because they make the balls fall downwards more slowly than if they were just dropped.

What is a wedge?

A ramp or **inclined plane** is usually placed on the ground. You use the slope to help you climb. It is the surface of the ramp that is important for the jobs it does.

A **wedge** is a different shape that looks like two solid ramps stuck together. A wedge is usually moved through something to do its job.

A wedge is a solid shape like two ramps stuck together.

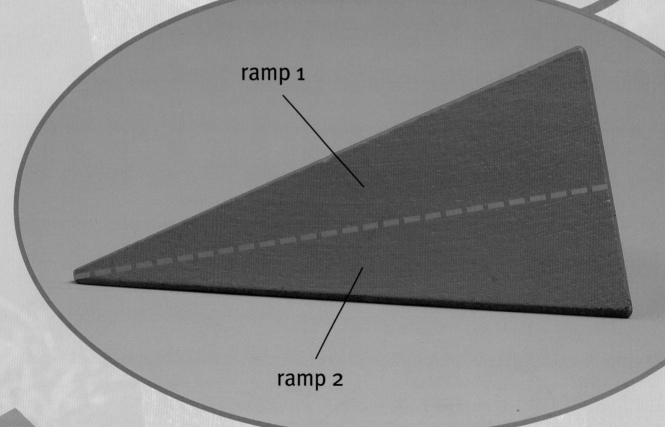

ramp 1

ramp 2

A wedge is a **simple machine** that helps to push things apart. By pushing the wide end of the wedge it moves downwards. As the wedge moves through the **material** the push downwards turns into a push outwards.

A wedge changes a forwards or downwards movement into an outwards movement. This happens because the wide part of the wedge is now in the material and pushing it apart.

push downwards

push outwards

push outwards

A hammer can be used to bash a wedge into something such as this tree trunk.

What does a wedge do?

Wedges are usually used to push things apart. An axe has a metal head with a narrow, sharp end and a wide end. An axe can be used to cut wood, which is a hard material.

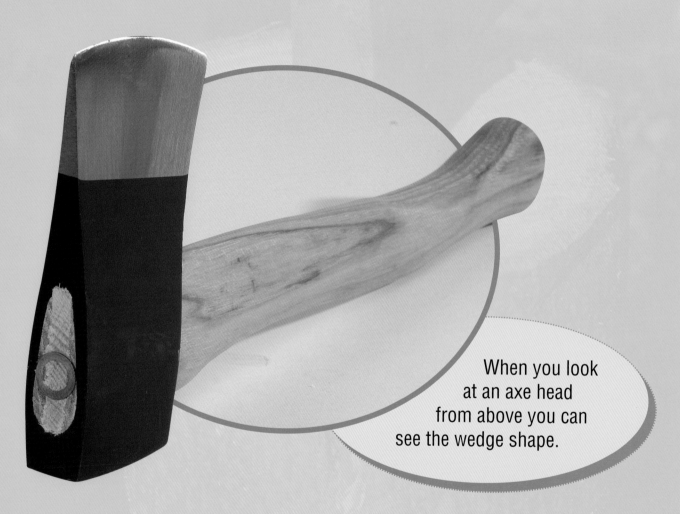

When you look at an axe head from above you can see the wedge shape.

What would happen without...?

The axe makes it possible for us to cut up trees. It would be almost impossible to cut open a tree trunk using just your hands.

Woodcutters use axes to chop up wood.

axe head (wedge)

handle (lever)

The head of an axe is joined to a handle, which gives you something to hold on to. The handle is also a **lever**. A lever is another **simple machine**.

When you swing an axe, the axe head moves a larger distance than the handle where you hold it. This makes the axe head move faster, so it can cut into things. An axe is a **compound machine**. A compound machine is something that uses two or more simple machines together.

Wedges in everyday life

Pins that hold up posters are also **wedges**. If you look at the pins closely you can see that they become very narrow at the end. A pin or needle is a sort of round wedge. It does not have just two slopes, but it works in the same way as an ordinary wedge.

These pins are tiny wedges. Can you see the wedge shape?

What would happen without...?

Without wedges in pins and needles, it would be a lot harder to push things into walls or through **material**. Imagine trying to push a pin without a point into a wall. Ouch!

A door wedge helps to hold a door open. When the door tries to close, it pushes against the wedge. The wedge shape pushes up against the bottom of the door, and down against the floor. This means there is a lot of **friction** between the wedge, the door, and the floor. The wedge will not move and the door stays open.

All the different pushes from the door and the wedge cause friction, which stops the door from moving.

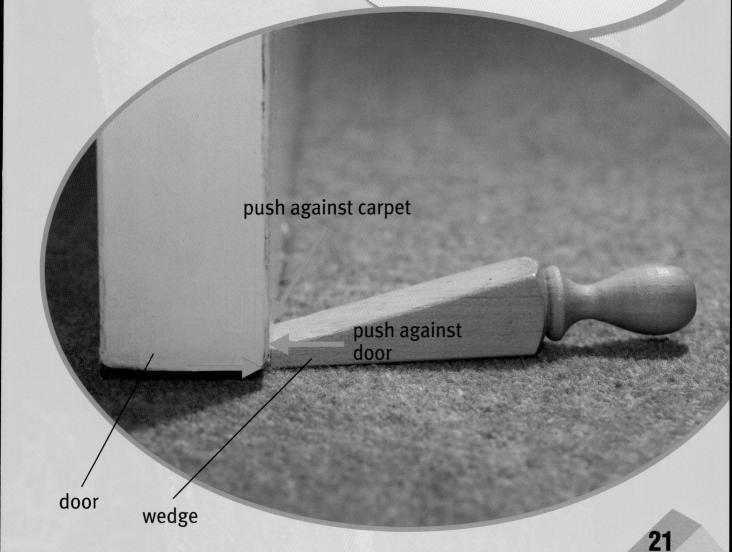

push against carpet

push against door

door

wedge

Wearing wedges

A zip is something that uses **wedges**. Look closely at a zip on your clothes, or on a bag. On either side of the zip you can see lots of small teeth. These teeth are special shapes that lock together to hold your clothes or bag shut.

The part of the zip that you pull to join the teeth together is called the slide.

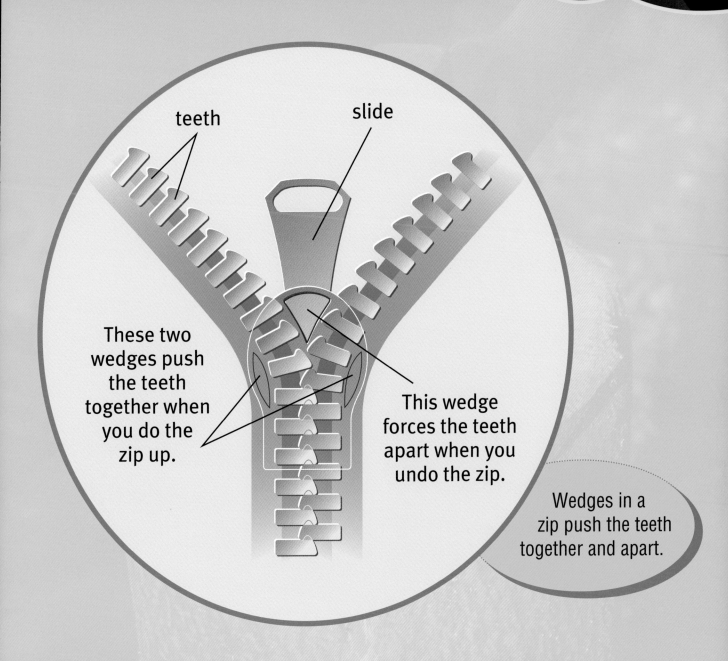

teeth

slide

These two wedges push the teeth together when you do the zip up.

This wedge forces the teeth apart when you undo the zip.

Wedges in a zip push the teeth together and apart.

The slide of a zip has three wedges inside it. The wedge at the top is triangle shaped and is used to push the teeth apart when you pull the zip down. The other two wedges are oval shaped. These wedges push the teeth together again when the zip is done up. When you pull the slide up they make the two sides of the zip lock together.

23

Wedges in machines

Farmers use **wedges** in a machine called a plough. A plough has lots of blades that cut through soil. Each blade is a wedge. As a tractor pulls the plough, the sharp ends of the blades dig into the soil. The blades are also sloped like a ramp. This lifts the soil up as well as pushing it apart.

tractor

plough

blade

Turning over all the soil in this field would be a tough job without the tractor and plough!

Boats and snowploughs use a wedge shape at the front. This helps them travel through water or snow. The wedge helps them move with less **effort force** because it pushes the water or snow out to the side.

Speedboats use a wedge to help them travel through water very quickly.

What would happen without...?

If a boat had a flat front, it would take a lot more effort force to move it through the water. It would not be able to go very quickly because the water would push straight up against it.

Living ramps and wedges

A shark's teeth are **wedges**. Like humans, sharks push their teeth together to bite into food. Sharks' teeth have tiny blades along the edges that help them to tear up their food.

Sharks and other fish have wedge-shaped bodies to help them swim smoothly and quickly through water.

Your front teeth are also wedge shaped. Feel how they are thicker at the top and thinner at the bottom. Your teeth are shaped so that you can bite into hard foods and pull small pieces into your mouth.

The big square teeth at the back of your mouth are not so good for biting. They are for grinding up the food that is already in your mouth.

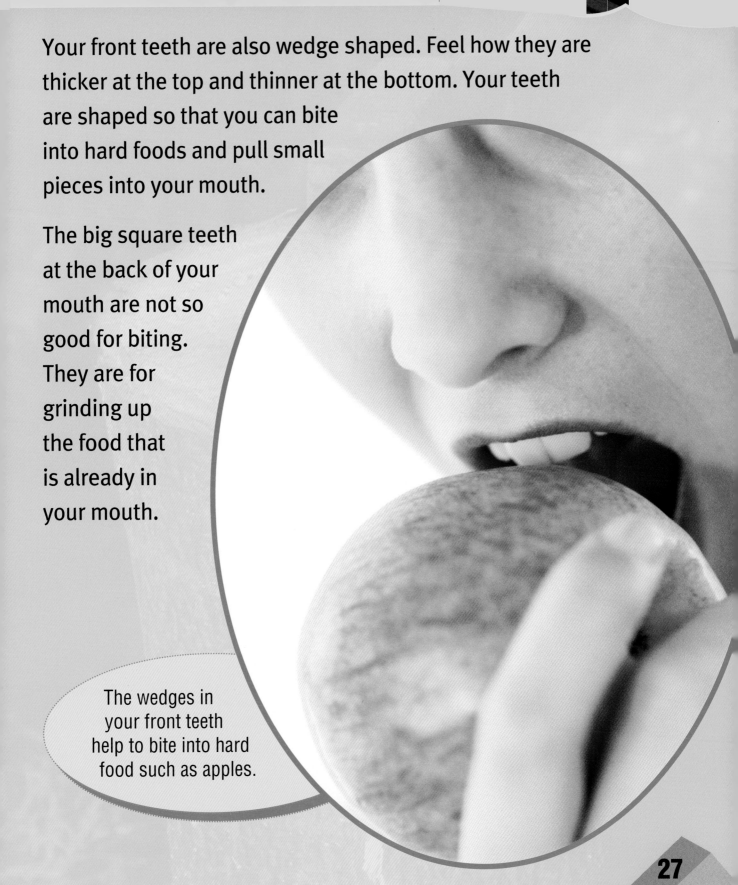

The wedges in your front teeth help to bite into hard food such as apples.

27

Ramps and wedges in machines

The blades of a pair of scissors are two **wedges**. These blades are fixed together like two **levers** to make a machine that cuts things. The levers let you close the handles at one end of the scissors. As you do this, the blades close together. Your **effort force** on the handles becomes a pushing down **force** on the blades. The blades then push the paper apart.

joined together
like levers

blades (wedges)

A pair of scissors uses wedges and levers together so it is a **compound machine**.

If you make a ramp and wrap it around a pole you get another very useful machine called a screw. When you turn a screw, the ramp shape up the side helps you to move the screw slowly into a surface. A screw is a **simple machine** that turns round and round movement into forwards and backwards movement.

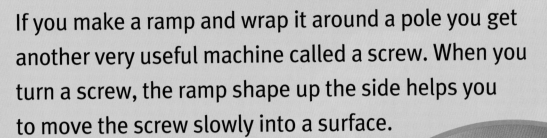

Screws are very useful machines that are used to hold things together.

Find out for yourself

You can find out about **simple machines** by talking to your teacher or parents. Think about the simple machines you use every day – how do you think they work? Your local library will have books and information about this. You will find the answers to many of your questions in this book, but you can also use other books and the Internet.

Books to read

Science Around Us: Pull and Push, Sally Hewitt
   (Chrysalis Children's Books, 2004)
Very Useful Machines: Ramps and Wedges,
   Chris Oxlade (Heinemann Library, 2003)
What do Ramps and Wedges do? David Glover
   (Heinemann Library, 2001)

Using the Internet

Explore the Internet to find out more about ramps and **wedges**. Try using a search engine such as www.yahooligans.com or www.internet4kids.com, and type in keywords such as 'ramp', 'wedge', and 'slope'.

Glossary

angle pointed space between two lines, or the corner of an object

axle rod that goes through the centre of a wheel or group of wheels

compound machine machine that uses two or more simple machines

effort force force that you put into a ramp or wedge

engine machine that can make things move

force push or pull. Forces can make things move.

friction something that happens when two surfaces rub against each other. Friction can slow things down or stop them moving.

gravity force that pulls everything towards the ground

inclined plane sloping surface or ramp

lever stiff bar or stick that moves around a fixed point called a fulcrum

material substance that can be used to make things. Wood, brick, plastic and paper are all examples of materials.

pulley rope or chain wrapped around a wheel and axle to help lift things up

simple machine something that can change the effort force needed to move something, or change the direction it moves in

vertical up and down

wedge two ramps joined together, back to back

Index